Gypsy Horses

Written and Illustrated by **Lise McNamara**

A *Moving On* Book

Publisher:
Robert Dawson/Derbyshire Gypsy Liaison Group

2004

Publisher Robert Dawson, on behalf of
Derbyshire Gypsy Liaison Group
188 Alfreton Road, Blackwell,
Alfreton, Derbys. DE55 5JH

ISBN 1-903418-53-4

RA 7.4
CA 8 to 14

Series editor Robert Dawson

Printed by 4 Sheets Design and Print
197 Mansfield Road, Nottingham, NG1 3FS

Gypsy Horses

MOVING ON series

Acknowledgement

From an idea suggested by
Wrexham Traveller Education Service.

Derbyshire Gypsy Liaison Group acknowledges with gratitude funding assistance given by the Esmee Fairbairn Foundation and by the Tudor Trust without whom these books would not have been possible.

Teachers' Note:
Youngsters may need assistance with the some
words/blends:

At the Blarney Stone Acres Ranch in New Jersey, Lise McNamara and her husband Steve and daughter Kelsey keep and breed horses which in the USA are known as Gypsy Horses or Gypsy Vanners. They are the type of horse kept and used by Travellers throughout Britain .

In the UK they are sometimes called Coloureds, Cobs, Grys, Vanners, and especially, Traveller horses.

Lise, Steve and Kelsey are unusual because in the whole of the USA there are only 500 Gypsy horses.

Lise says, *"We are so proud of these horses. They have a quality of elegance, beauty, and movement that is incredible. They are unlike any other breed of horse."*

Now read on . . .

Gypsy Horses

We're proud of Gypsy Horses. That's the name we in the USA call these very well bred horses. We also call them Gypsy Vanners. The word Vanner was chosen to honour the horses that pull the old wagons. In England they are called black and whites cobs and grys. In this book, we will call them Gypsy Horses.

Gypsy Horses come in many colours, shapes and sizes. The most popular colours are black and white and brown and white. They are called piebald and skewbald. Some horses are solid and some are tri-coloured black, brown and white. The most prized colour is the black and white. Some are pony size and some are horse size.

They have beautiful long manes and tails. The hair on their legs helps to protect their feet. This hair is called feathering. The hair on their manes and tails and faces help to protect them from insects. They can use their tails to swipe the bugs away. The hair is to protect them and we think it makes them beautiful.

Gypsy Horses have great temperaments for children and adults. They are easy to handle and they are easy to train. They are very friendly horses and really enjoy the company of humans. They have excellent movement and can excel at many equestrian sports.

In Ireland, many people ride the horses for sport. They can jump and go long distances.

In England, many Travelling people used these horses to pull their wagons. They had to be very strong for this and have lots of good bone. You need a horse with good temperament to use in traffic. A very quiet and sensible horse is important when driving around trucks and cars. Safety is very important.

We use these horses for driving and riding in the USA. They make very good horses for children because they are so calm. Some people like to ride in an English saddle for sports like jumping or dressage. They can also be ridden in a Western saddle that is a heavier saddle with a horn on the front of it. The cowboys use this horn for roping cattle.

Even though the horses seem very heavy, they can move gracefully. They are light on their feet and very comfortable to ride. They are very flexible and can bend very easily so they are good for many kinds of riding. Some people like to ride dressage because of how flexible they are and the way their feet move naturally. When they walk their back foot reaches their front foot. This is a very desirable trait. It is often called "tracking up" and is an indicator of excellent condition.

Many people take the time to train these horses, but children can just hop on their backs and ride. This is because they are so easy and calm. This calmness makes them a safe horse to use and they are so strong they can carry a couple of grown men on their backs without any problem.

In the United States, people use them for driving competitions. In Ireland, they excel in jumping and cross-country events. In order to compete, they must clip the feathering on the legs and they shorten their manes. For people in the states the more feathering and the longer the mane the better. Therefore, we like to leave their manes and feathering alone. We like a more natural look.

They are a new horse to the United States and they are becoming very popular. They are being shown in breed exhibitions all around the country. People are very curious about this horse.

In all Europe, there are only about three thousand, which is still not a large number.

These horses have very strong hoofs. In the United Sates, we do not put shoes on them unless we are using them to pull carriages. If you are riding them on a street, you need the shoes to protect their feet. Their feet must be cleaned out with a hoof pick so they do not get any stones or decay in them. Stones and decay can cause lameness. Taking care of your horse's feet is very important. If a horse has a sore or lame foot, you cannot ride it.

A farrier comes and trims their feet to keep their feet healthy. The farrier can also put horseshoes on if it is needed. He measures their feet and he heats the iron shoe up so he can form the shoe to fit their feet. If you do not take care of your horse's feet, you will not have a good horse. Not many people can be a farrier. It is a special job. You must know what you are doing or you could hurt the horse's feet instead of helping.

In England, they are often tied on the side of the road to graze. This is called tethering. In the United States, they put them in paddocks, which are fenced areas so that the horses cannot wander around. Some places have large turnouts for the horses. Others do not. The most important thing is for your horse to move around and get exercise.

Twice a day hay is brought in to feed the horses. Pellets can also be fed twice daily to give the horses the nutrition they need. A couple of flakes of hay twice daily and a half a scoop of pellets is enough to feed these horses as they are what we call very "easy keepers".

England has lots of grass and the soil has many minerals, which are good for them. In the United States, many people do not have rich fields of grass so we buy hay for them to eat. There are farmers who cut and bale the hay so we can buy it to feed our horses. Sometimes our hay is hard to get so we give the horse pellets, which is a man-made food for them. We also give them supplements because our soil does not have the vitamins and minerals that they need.

Most horses like to be kept together in a bunch or a herd. Sometimes horses fight and you need to separate them. Many times a stallion (male horse) will fight with the other horses so they are kept separate. Gypsy horses usually get along well and they can all be kept together.

These horses are very easy to care for. They can stay out in all kinds of weather. They have beautiful coats to protect them. They don't mind the rain or snow; in fact, they like the snow. They will stand out in it until the snow covers them. Snow actually is an insulator and it protects them. Horses really like the cold weather better than the heat. They have more energy in the cold weather.

Sometimes they are kept in a barn, which has stalls to keep them out of the weather. A barn with stalls can house a few horses at the same time. Sometimes people keep them outside and give them protection from the weather with a lean-to or a shelter.

We like to give horses a shelter, which is made of wood with a roof to help protect them from the snow and rain. Horses have flight instinct. When they are scared, they run. Many horses will not use a shelter because of this flight instinct. When they are in a shelter, they cannot see around them, so they prefer to be outside where they can see everything.

Gypsy horses are very smart. When it is cold and the water freezes, they use their feet to break the ice to get at the water. They also use their feet to dig in the snow to look for food. They will also use their mouth and teeth and they like to chew things. Often they will chew on trees and logs.

Horses are very curious creatures. If they are left alone and ignored, they get bored. They can develop bad habits like kicking, chewing or calling out for other horses. It is good if they have trees or logs in their pasture to keep them busy. They like to be with other horses to play. They really like to be with their owners because they like people so much. Some horses would rather be with their owners instead of other horses. This trait is characteristic of the breed.

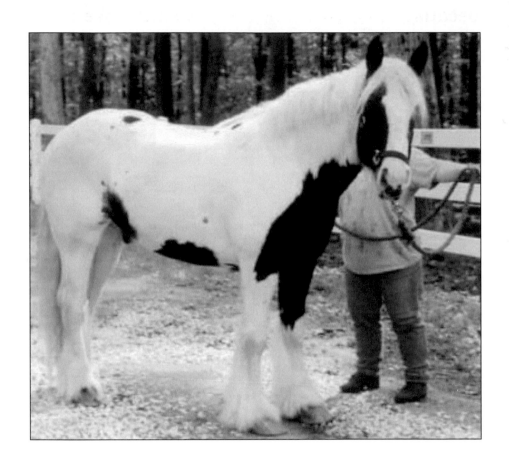

We try to time the birth of the foal to coordinate with the weather. In the United States, foals can be born earlier in the year because they can be housed in barns. We can also add lamps to the stalls to give the new foal warmth. In England, many foals are born out in a field and mares have their foals all by themselves. They just leave the herd and find a quiet place to deliver their foal. Because the weather can be bad, many people try to plan the birth of the foal in the late spring or early summer. Most Gypsy foals are born between April and July.

Mares and stallions are cleaned before they are bred so they don't carry any infections. Once the mare is pregnant, we try to keep her quiet for thirty days. During her pregnancy, the vet gives her shots to protect the foal from any diseases. Other than that, there is no special care for her until the last three months of pregnancy. In the last three months, the mare gets extra food for her and for her growing foal. It takes about eleven months before the mare can deliver her new foal. For humans it takes nine months.

At three hundred days of pregnancy, we watch the mare closely. We look for signs of the up-coming birth. The mare's udder will start to fill up with milk in order to prepare for the new foal. When we see the mare is almost ready, we bring her inside into a stall. We put down straw for the delivery. Straw is not dusty so we don't have to worry about it getting into their nose or mouth. It is also absorbent and soft for the foal to be born on.

When foals are born, it is very exciting. It can happen very quickly, usually in a half an hour or less. Because it happens so fast, we often miss the birth of the foal. It is always a surprise to see what the new foal will look like. With these horses, you never know what color it will be. The Gypsy horses have no set colour genetics for breeding. Any colour horse can produce any colour foal.

Because horses are born with a flight instinct, it is only a matter of minutes before the foals are up and running. This is a necessary instinct because in the wild they might have to get away quickly from predators. New mums are very protective with their foals. They watch over them carefully. New foals stay very close to their mothers.

Foals drink milk from their mums. They imitate everything that their mum does. Very quickly, they learn to eat grass or hay and drink water. By the time they are two weeks old their teeth come in and they can eat solid food. This is a very important time for the foal because they learn all their habits from their mother.

When the foals are between four and six months, we separate them from their mums. This is also called weaning. Some people just take them away. The less stressful way is to have mares and foals together. Every day we take one mare away from the group. This way the foals always have the security of the group. The foals enjoy the company of the other horses. They love to wrestle and play with each other.

They are important to Gypsy families for their livelihood. In addition, there are taken care of very well. It is a great source of pride to own a good Gypsy horse. They are often compared to gold. Many breeders will hide their horses away so that they cannot easily be found by their competition.

In the States, we are putting microchips in our horses. We also take hair samples so they can be DNA tested. This is done because they are valuable and if they are stolen, we can prove our ownership. These horses can be very expensive.

Most of our horses come from England. Before they leave England, a vet checks them. After they are approved to leave the country, they fly these horses over on airplanes. The horses don't seem to mind. Once they are here, they have to go into quarantine. Quarantine is a place where they isolate the horses so that they won't bring any diseases in to the country. It is two days quarantine for geldings and horses under the age of two. If it is a mare over the age of two, she has to stay for two weeks in quarantine. A stallion stays for six weeks to make sure he is free of disease.

Here at Blarney Stone Acres, we worked very hard to find the best quality Gypsy horses to start our breeding program. We picked four mares from some of the best family owned stock in England. We had them checked by a veterinarian in England. They were taken by ferry to The Netherlands (Holland) and then flown to one of the biggest airports in the United States called JFK. This airport is named after John F. Kennedy a former US president.

Now that they are home with us, we are so proud of these horses. They have a quality of elegance, beauty, and movement that is incredible. We plan to continue to breed in the Gypsy tradition and hope to make our friends in the UK proud of us. We thank our friends not only for producing such incredible horse but also for sharing them with us. They are a breed unlike any other breed. They are a horse that people dream of owning. Every time we look at them it takes our breath away.

Although we have had other horses over the years we have found the Gypsy horses the easiest horses to work with. If you keep a horse at a barn and they take care of it for you, it is not the same as taking care of them your self. If you have years of riding experience, the real knowledge comes from working with your horse every day. You learn to deal with all kinds of temperament, training and any basic medical you need to know on an everyday basis. The real learning experience is hands on experience.

We are proud owners and breeders of the Gypsy horse.

Index

The Moving On Series

100+ Culture-specific books for Traveller children

Pre-school/Toddler
4 planned

Key Stage 1
1 available, more planned

Key Stage 1 and 2
2 available, more planned

Key Stage 2
4 available, more planned

Key Stage 3
2 available, more planned

Available from DGLG,
Ernest Bailey Community Centre,
New Street,
Matlock,
Derbys.
DE4 3FE

OR

Publisher.